"A superhero to rival all other superheroes! We are all in need of heroes. None more than those that have difficulties with managing frustrations, anxiety, anger, emotional regulation, and the ins and outs of sensory processing. Lauren Brukner stands at the forefront of her profession and presents this book as a beacon of hope and a positive force in the lives of both children and the adults that care for them. By breaking down and simplifying such complex issues into small digestible bits, the text is instantly entertaining and enlightening all at once."

—Dr. Frederick B. Covington, OTD

"Lauren Brukner's relatable narrative and pictures put words to charged emotions and feelings, empowering students with strategies to conquer them... Be prepared to 'Throw your Worries Away!'"

—Beverly Moskowitz, DOT, MS OTR/L FAOTA,
CEO at Real OT Solutions, Inc.

"This book places the child in charge, providing them with tools and strategies. It uses a superhero figure to guide the child, giving them useful, practical and fun ways of coping and managing, helping them in turn to become their own self-help genie, find their inner guru, and become their own expert, feeling instructor."

—Alice Cruttwell, Shropshire Public Health Curriculum Advisor, author of the award winning Shropshire Respect Yourself programme and key contributor to the PSHE Association primary Mental Health curriculum

by the same author

The Kids' Guide to Staying Awesome and In Control
Simple Stuff to Help Children Regulate their Emotions and Senses
Illustrated by Apsley
ISBN 978 1 84905 997 8
eISBN 978 0 85700 962 3

of related interest

Starving the Anger Gremlin for Children Aged 5–9
A Cognitive Behavioural Therapy Workbook on Anger Management
Kate Collins-Donnelly
ISBN 978 1 84905 493 5
eISBN 978 0 85700 885 5

Starving the Anxiety Gremlin for Children Aged 5–9
A Cognitive Behavioural Therapy Workbook on Anxiety Management
Kate Collins-Donnelly
ISBN 978 1 84905 492 8
eISBN 978 0 85700 902 9

The Panicosaurus
Managing Anxiety in Children Including Those with Asperger Syndrome
K.I. Al-Ghani
Illustrated by Haitham Al-Ghani
ISBN 978 1 84905 356 3
eISBN 978 0 85700 706 3

Anger Management Games for Children
Deborah M. Plummer
Illustrated by Jane Serrurier
ISBN 978 1 84310 628 9
eISBN 978 1 84642 775 6

HOW TO BE A
SUPERHERO CALLED
SELF-CONTROL!

Super Powers to Help Younger Children
to Regulate their Emotions and Senses

LAUREN BRUKNER
ILLUSTRATED BY APSLEY

Jessica Kingsley *Publishers*
London and Philadelphia

First published in 2016
by Jessica Kingsley Publishers
73 Collier Street
London N1 9BE, UK
and
400 Market Street, Suite 400
Philadelphia, PA 19106, USA

www.jkp.com

Library of Congress Cataloging in Publication Data
Brukner, Lauren.
  How to be a superhero called self-control! : super powers to help younger children
to regulate their emotions and senses / Lauren Brukner ; illustrated by Apsley.
     pages cm
  ISBN 978-1-84905-717-2 (alk. paper)
 1. Self-control in children--Juvenile literature. 2. Emotions in children--Juvenile
literature. 3. Child psychology--Juvenile literature. I. Apsley, illustrator. II. Title.
  BF723.S25B777 2016
  155.42'3825--dc23
                          2015018546

British Library Cataloguing in Publication Data
A CIP catalogue record for this book is available from the British Library.

ISBN 978 1 84905 717 2
eISBN 978 1 78450 203 4

Manufactured by Thomson-Shore, Dexter, MI (USA); RMA91HS55, November, 2015

This book is dedicated to all children, everywhere. Know that you are all superheroes, amazingly powerful, unique, and wonderful, just the way you are. My wish for you is to just believe it, mind, heart, and soul.

Acknowledgments

As always, I am so thankful to my commissioning editor, Rachel Menzies, whose endless hard work, patience, and belief in the vision of this work has helped to develop it from an idea into the book that you are reading at this very moment. Words cannot express my gratitude. I also thank the amazing editorial staff and marketing team at Jessica Kingsley Publishers. I feel so blessed to work with a company that values the benefit of publishing books that make a difference in the lives of others.

To Adele Schroeter, Alison Porcelli, and Gabriel Feldberg: I couldn't have asked for better colleagues, friends, and cheerleaders. Your dedication, hard work, and devotion to the children in your school is inspiring. It is such a privilege to work alongside you. To the amazingly hardworking, devoted, and talented educational and therapeutic team of teachers and service providers at PS 59 with whom I have had the privilege of working over the years: I could not have written this book without you. I am so grateful to call you not only my coworkers but also my friends. (I wish that I could name you all, but it would take too many pages!)

To the parents and children with whom I have worked over the many years that I have practiced: You have been my teachers. I have learned so much, and I am blessed to continue to have so many of you in my life. To the parents, teachers, related service providers, and of course children who I have not had the pleasure to meet (yet!): Know that I have been there, in so many ways. As a therapist and as a mom, I applaud you. You are amazing. Realize it, each and every day.

To all of my amazing friends, near and far, thanks for the love and support. You rock.

To my wonderful parents: Thank you so much for providing me with the tools, love, and drive to know that yes, I could write if I just believed that I could. To my sister: You are my best friend, always and forever. Your belief in me as a writer has gotten me so far. To my brilliant in-laws: I could not have written this book without you. Your support, love, and help over the years has allowed me to follow this dream. To the love of my life, Joel: Thank you for tolerating the computer light in your face at all hours, my "I can't talk I'm writing," and for your continuous and unwavering love and support. You are my soul mate. Lastly, to my three little loves: You are my life. You are the reason I do it all. Realize that if you work hard enough, and want it hard enough, you can follow your dreams and accomplish more than you would have thought possible.

Contents

PART 1

FOR KIDS

All About Me: Self-Control!

So, I know some pretty famous superheroes. They're pretty cool guys (and girls). They even take me along when they do cool stuff like swinging across buildings and flying through the air! I've gotten less scared during the flying parts, mostly by not looking down.

Happy Harry? What? You haven't heard of him? Hmm, I won't tell him. Well, he is super-strong, and (shh...don't tell anybody), we are working together on some of his anger issues so he can feel calm and happy, even when things don't go his way. You must know Lightning Lizzy! No? Are you sure? Well, she must be going too fast for you to see her! It's awesome to be able to go at the speed of light to save, well, the world, but I've been helping her slow down a bit, when she has a moment. Hmm, who else of my superhero buddies might you know? Oh, I got it! Stretchy Sue! She can bend and stretch into all kinds of shapes. The last time I saw her, she was helping out Happy Harry as she was curled up into a human pretzel! Seriously. Something that I have been helping her with is being a little flexible in her thinking, not just her body! Kind of funny, no? She can bend and flex in all kinds of ways with her arms and legs, but she doesn't like to be flexible when it comes to things like sharing or doing something another person's way!

And then there's me. Yep, that's right, down there. I'm a superhero, too. See the totally awesome cape, mask, and watch? Yep. Pretty cool, huh?

My name is **Self-Control**. Have you heard of me? Maybe not. I'm not in any comics, and I haven't starred in any movies (yet). I'm more of an "on-the-sidelines" kinda dude.

Have you ever been in a situation where you felt a really "yucky" feeling, but you somehow got the strength and *control* to feel better? Guess what? I may have been there, whispering my secrets to you!

Well, maybe, maybe not. I lose track of all the kids (and grownups) that I help all over the world. It's an exhausting job… no weekends, no vacations, very little sleep…but *somebody's* gotta do it.

So, here's my job, in a nutshell: My super power is, obviously, getting kids to feel like **super self-control experts**! Being able to get rid of any of the yucky feelings that can pop up during the day (or night), with my simple bag of super powers. Now's not the time to be modest. I'm quite the expert. So much so, in fact, that **Self-Control** is my superhero name, after all. But, my friends, how does this help *you*?

Frankly, I'm tired. It's getting a little exhausting having to fly to the many situations where I am needed 24/7, across the globe. The first few times—eating gelato in Milan, sushi in Tokyo, and deep-dish pizza in Chicago, all in one day—was quite exciting. (Yes, I can fly that fast.)

Now, I just want to have some down time. Maybe some sleeping in on the weekends, curled up on the couch with a good book, without the ever-sounding BEEP of my self-control alarm watch going off every minute or so.

It's time, my friends, to pass the torch. Let me teach you what I know so that you can become like me, **Self-Control**! (Maybe you can even wear a cape.) Wait. You already have one? I'll bet it's not the same as mine!

How This Book Works

Are you ready to be a detective? Great! Put on your detective hat. Make sure it's nice and tight. Pull it down until it feels just right. Perfect. Now reach deep, deep, deep, into your pocket. Look—there's a magnifying glass! Now we are ready to figure out how to help these kids, solve their problems, and learn my simple bag of super powers!

It's really kind of magical. Seriously. Don't believe me? You'll see for yourself soon enough. If we do the tip or trick the right way, we help the character in the picture!

If we don't, well, good luck, character.

So, let's try our best, shall we? (Trust me, I can tell if you are faking it. **Self-Control** powers, remember?)

Are you ready? Thumbs up if you are. OK, let's start!

Frustration

All of the scenes that we are going to look at first have kids who feel **frustrated**. Do you know what "frustrated" means? When someone feels frustrated, they may feel upset or annoyed, especially if they can't change something or do something the way they want.

Do you have a tip that has worked for you when you felt this way? What made you feel better? If you feel comfortable sharing this, touch your nose quietly. That will show the grownup reading this book that you want to talk about it.

Super Power #1: Take a Deep Breath!

David is playing a board game with his brother. His brother gets the last piece in, to make four in a row. His brother wins the game. Now David is frustrated. He slams the table in frustration and yells, "This is too hard! You always win!"

Let's learn how to help David feel better together, OK? Go teamwork!

The first step in learning to be, well, like me, is to learn to **Take a Deep Breath!** That's right, a deep breath. But hey, it's harder than it sounds! Let's have some fun with this one!

OK, close your eyes. Pretend that you have a jar filled with bubbles. Do you feel its weight in your hand? Is it slippery? Make sure to hold onto it tightly! Good. Now, unscrew the cap and pull out the wand. Is it wet? It's OK if it is, just brush it off.

(That's called being flexible, another **Self-Control** awesome thing that we will get to.)

Does your bubble wand have enough soap on it? If not, give it another dip in the bubbles. Good, we are all ready.

Now, breathe in slowly through your nose. When you blow out, you are going to blow a bubble as big as the room you are in, as big as the grownup reading this to you (that's pretty big, huh?).

Remember, if you breathe too softly, you won't make any bubbles, and if you breathe too fast or too hard, the bubble will pop!

Let's turn the page and see if we helped David! (I hope so; board games are fun. It would be a shame for him to not enjoy playing them.)

Super Power #2: Make a Mantra!

Still have your detective hat on? Great! We're on to our next case.

Lily looks at her friends at the arts center drawing pictures of their families. Her hand is hurting, and she doesn't know how to make her picture look like theirs. She rips up her picture and throws it in the garbage. Her teacher comes over and asks her why she did that. "I can't draw. My pictures look like scribble scrabble!"

Let's learn how to help Lily feel better together, OK? Go teamwork!

Ready for Super Power #2? OK, it sounds kind of funny. It's called **Make a Mantra!** What is that silly word? Well, I'll tell you…

When I get frustrated, there are certain words and sentences that I like to tell myself over and over, that make me feel better. For example, if I lose the flying races games at the Superhero Olympics, I tell myself "No big deal!" or "Oh well, maybe next time!"

Think of something that happened recently that may have made you feel frustrated. Show a silent thumbs up when you have that moment in your mind. OK, great!

Let's practice saying a few mantras:

"Oh well, maybe next time!"

"No big deal!"

"I can try again another time!"

"I am awesome no matter what!"

"I am loved!"

Which is your favorite? Show a silent thumbs up so the adult reading this book knows you have one in your mind. If you want, share it with them.

Let's turn the page and see if we helped Lily! (I hope so; I would love for her to feel confident that she can draw! Even if it's different from what her friends are drawing.)

Super Power #3: Use Your Words!

So you've accomplished your first superhero tasks. You have mastered the first two super powers: **Take a Deep Breath!** and **Make a Mantra!** Give yourself a pat on the back. Great job! You have taken the first two steps to being, well, like me!

OK, **Self-Control**, focus, focus! Let's all look at the picture.

Ray is waiting for his turn on the slide. Just as he is about to slide down, another boy pushes him out of the way and slides down first. "Um, um...," Ray stammers, but, to his frustration, no words come out.

Ray is having trouble using his words. Can you think of a time when you had lots of thoughts and feelings in your head, but couldn't explain to others (or yourself!) how you felt? It can be pretty frustrating, can't it? I have felt that way, too (yep, even me). What made you feel better? If you feel comfortable sharing this, touch your nose quietly. That will show the grownup reading this book that you want to talk about it.

Maybe Ray took a deep breath like we learned about, but he is having trouble telling himself or a grownup how he is feeling.

When you have felt frustrated, have you heard somebody tell you, "**Use your words!**"? That can feel hard, especially if you are feeling sad, mad, or another kind of bad feeling. I'll be honest:

It *is* important to use your words to explain how you feel, at least to *yourself*, and maybe to a grownup who can help you, so that you can feel better. When you use your words, a helpful grownup can help make whatever feels hard easier for you.

Let's practice the next super power: **Use Your Words!**

Close your eyes, and **take a deep breath** like we practiced (no cheating...I'll know, trust me). Now, I want you to think about how you are feeling in this moment. Are you happy? Peaceful? Tired? Are you frustrated, sad, or angry? Maybe you are a mixture of many different feelings, and that's OK. When you have your feeling clear in your mind, give a thumbs up. Use your words to tell the adult who is reading this book how you are feeling.

OK, back to Ray. Let's see if using this new super power, **Use Your Words!** helped Ray use his own words to tell his friend that it was *his* turn on the slide! Turn the page and see what we find.

Anxiety

All of the scenes that we are going to look at now have kids who feel **anxious** or **worried**. Do you know what it means to feel anxious or worried? When someone feels anxious or worried, they may feel nervous about a number of things. For example, you may feel worried about something that may happen. You may be worried, or anxious, if you are not sure what to expect. You may feel worried in your thoughts and also in your body. Your heart may beat quickly. Your stomach may not feel right. Your head may hurt. Other parts of your body may also feel pretty yucky. Have you ever had the same worrisome thoughts over and over again? Do they pop into your head, even when you are trying your best to just not think about them? Some kids may try to stay away from people, places, or things that make them feel anxious or worried—but then they are usually missing out on the best parts of life! Feeling anxious or worried can be really tough.

Do you have a tip that has worked for you when you have felt this way? What made you feel better? If you feel comfortable sharing this, touch the top of your head quietly. That will show the grownup reading this book that you want to talk about it.

Super Power #4: Just Give Yourself a Hug!

Talk about super! You guys are amazing! Give yourselves a pat on the back for jobs well done. I know you can help Joseph, the next kid who needs our help.

Joseph does not like fire drills. Every day, he comes in and asks his teacher, "Are we having a fire drill today?" His teacher is very good at telling him when there will be one, so that Joseph can feel less nervous when the loud ringing starts and he has to go with his class down the hallway quickly and line up outside. "It's just practice," his teacher reminds him. One day, the fire alarm rings! Joseph feels so scared! He didn't hear about it from his teacher. He starts yelling and hides under his desk. "Help, help!" Joseph screams.

Oh no, we have to get Joseph out of that building and keep him and his class practicing safe fire drill behavior!

Are you ready? Off we go!

Ready for Super Power #4? OK, it's one I use myself whenever I get **scared**. (Bunny rabbits are one of those animals that make me scared, OK? Stop laughing! I hear you through the book!) The super power is…**Just Give Yourself a Hug!**

Think of something that happened recently that made you feel nervous, scared, or afraid. Show a silent thumbs up when you have that moment in your mind. OK, great!

Now, close your eyes. Think of a place where you feel the most peaceful and happy. Mine is cuddling with my parents under soft blankets on the couch in the living room, and sipping hot chocolate. I can picture the softness of the blanket and how cuddly my parents feel, the sweetness of my hot chocolate on my tongue, and hear their heartbeats as I lay on their chests.

Back to you. What's your moment? Thumbs up when you've got it. Now, reach out your arms and hug that moment tight so it stays in your heart. Remember, whenever you feel scared, that moment is right there, in your heart. You can always touch your chest, or do this super power again to feel peaceful, so you don't feel scared anymore.

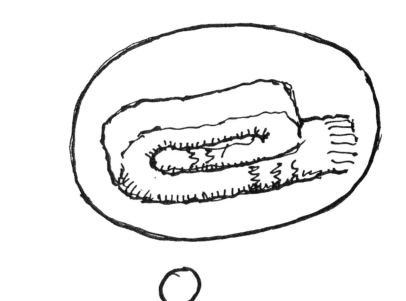

Let's see if doing **Just Give Yourself a Hug!** helped Joseph feel better and get out of the building feeling calm and safe…

Super Power #5: Crumple Up Your Worries!

Oh, gosh, boys and girls! Our friend Lianna needs our help.

Lianna is sitting up in her bed, hugging her stuffed bear close and crying. Her sheets are tossed around her. Her hair is in a tangle. She has bags under her eyes. Her mom rushes into the room. "Mommy, I had a bad dream! I'm scared!" Her mom rubs her back and whispers, "Go back to sleep, you're safe." Lianna just cries louder. "I can't! I'm just too scared to sleep!"

Do you like to crumple things? I sure do! I love to crumple all types of things: newspaper, construction paper, tissue paper… you name it. It feels great! You are going to really like our next super power, **Crumple Up Your Worries!**

Close your eyes. Picture in your mind a piece of paper and a marker. What color is the paper? What color is the marker? In your mind, draw out something that makes you feel scared. Don't leave anything out! You can even scribble scrabble if that makes you feel better! Now, take your fists and crumple that paper into the smallest ball that you can make. Now, whatever made you worried or scared is gone!

Let's see if doing **Crumple Up Your Worries!** helped Lianna fall back asleep…

Super Power #6: Throw Away Your Worries!

Everybody is afraid of something, right? Take me, for example. I'm afraid of teddy bears. (Don't you laugh at me, I can hear you through the book!) I'm also afraid of loud noises. It's hard for me to go to the movies, even though I absolutely love movies. I have to use a few of my super powers to get used to the noise and stop being afraid of it, so that I can actually enjoy the movie. What are you afraid of? If you feel like sharing, raise your right knee and the adult reading will know that you want to share.

OK, this gets us to our next kid who needs our help. Guess what? He's also afraid of noise!

"The noise! The noise!" Victor's ears are ringing, and the sound of the train screeching on the tracks is making his whole body hurt. It is scary. It feels like the noise is coming from inside of him! He covers his ears very tightly, but it just can't block the

noise! There is nowhere for him to go. "Mommy!" His mother rubs his back, hugging him tightly. "It can't hurt you, we are almost off. Don't worry," she says over and over, her voice loud, trying to carry over the screeching of the train. Victor can't hear her words, the noises are just too loud!

Wow, I definitely understand how Victor feels. Can you? OK, let's learn a new super power that can help Victor out. Ready? Let's go!

This super power is called **Throw Away Your Worries!** Here's what we are going to do:

Look around the room. Where is a good place that you would want to throw away your **worries**? Do you want to throw them out the window? Into the garbage can? Toward the door? What about the back of the chair? Once you know where you will throw your worries, wiggle your fingers. Now, close your eyes. Where do you feel your worries the most? Are they in your heart? Your belly? Your head? A mixture? What color are your worries? Can you picture them in your mind? Great. Now, grab your worries from wherever they are, hold onto them, and throw every bit of your worries away to the place that you chose to throw them. Phew. Doesn't that feel better?

Do you think that we helped Victor feel better about the noise on the train? I hope so!

Super Power #7: Make a Worry Box!

Dust off that detective hat and wipe your magnifying glass clean! We have more rescuing to do!

Shayna is coming back to school for the first day after winter vacation. She knows her friends in her class, but suddenly she feels afraid to go into the classroom. It just doesn't feel as familiar as it did before she went on winter break. Her teacher stands by the door: "Welcome back, boys and girls! Come on in!" Shayna's feet feel glued to the floor. She puts her backpack in front of her and starts crying and shaking.

Can I tell you a secret? I don't like coming back to superhero work after I go on short trips and vacations. It feels kind of scary, almost like I forgot parts of my job. Parts of my office feel less familiar, less safe. I understand how Shayna feels, don't you? Thumbs up if you understand this feeling.

I'll bet you've had these feelings at times, right? All of us have…even superheroes. (Just don't get the word out on that part. It's not good for the superhero business.)

Let's learn how to help Shayna feel better together, OK? You really are super.

The next super power we are going to use is called **Make a Worry Box!** "A what?" you may ask. That's right, a **Worry Box**. Let's learn how to make one…*in our minds*.

Close your eyes. Now, I want you to create a box where you are going to put away all of your worries, anything that you are afraid of, and lock it so that not even one tiny worry can escape. What does your **Worry Box** look like? Is it colorful? Is it smooth or rough? Have it in your mind? Now, put every single drop of anything that's worrying you right now into your **Worry Box**…make sure to get it all! Now, carefully close the lid and lock it tightly. There we go. Now, those worries are locked away and can't bother us; we don't have to think about them anymore. They're gone!

Do you think that using our **Make a Worry Box!** super power helped Shayna feel safe and happy enough to go into her classroom? Let's find out!

Sensory Processing

All of the scenes that we are going to look at now have kids who feel **wiggly**. Do you know what "wiggly" means? When someone feels wiggly, that's their body's way of saying: "Hey, I've been sitting still for too long! I need to move!" Do you have a part of your body where you feel wiggly the most? Some kids do, some kids don't. It's OK, either way. As for me, I usually feel wiggly in my hands and feet. After a while, they just start moving—well, that is, until I do my next super-amazing super power that you are now going to learn about!

Do you have a tip that has worked for you when you felt this way? What made you feel better? If you feel comfortable sharing this, wiggle your body in your seat. (Quietly…not too silly! I can see you over there! OK, it's not *that* funny!) That will show the grownup reading this book that you want to talk about it.

Super Power #8: Push Your Wiggles!

OK, boys and girls. Are you ready to get moving? That's right, we're going to do some exercise. Flex our muscles. Stretch our bodies. And do you want to know *why*? Of course you do. It's because these super powers, my super friends, are specially designed to help kids (and grownups) in need of getting out their wiggles in super-fun and super-simple ways!

Let's see who needs our help. Put your palms together, and let's dive into the picture!

It is time for a morning meeting. Ron is sitting on his rug spot, along the perimeter of the rug. He is trying so very hard to keep his body still, but it's just too hard! His back and neck are hurting, and his legs feel sticky as if they have minds of their own. Ron's hands and feet start to tap, quietly at first before getting louder and louder until his teacher taps him and whispers, "Please control your body." But how? Ron wonders, the wiggly feeling making him feel that he is about to burst.

Have you ever felt like Ron? I sure have. Wiggle your left thumb if you've felt that way. (I'll bet you have, even if you aren't wiggling it. I'm Self-Control, remember? I just know these things.)

Ready to help? Great! The super power we are about to try is called **Push Your Wiggles!** Scoop up all the **wiggles** in your body. Start at your toes and go all the way up to your head. Hold them in your hands. Have you got all of them? Great. Now, here's where it gets a little tricky. Pay close attention. Cross one arm over the other arm, so that your hands are on your shoulders (still closed and holding your wiggles). Now, open up your hands and **push** down on your shoulders, making those wiggles disappear! Magic!

What do you think? Was our **Push Your Wiggles!** exercise enough to help Ron sit and listen to his teacher? Let's find out!

Super Power #9: Squeeze Your Wiggles!

Can I ask you a question? Do you ever have days where you feel like you sat for such a long, long time and didn't get to move enough? I sure have. Once, I went to a superheroes conference that lasted for eight hours! They only let us get up for 30 minutes! Imagine sitting for that long! I won't be going back there for a while, that's for sure—not even for the delicious free pizza!

Who else do we have who is having some wiggly troubles? Wipe your magnifying glasses. Are they clean? Great!

Jessica is eating dinner with her family. Her sister, mother, and father are sitting at the table, eating while they talk about their day. Jessica cannot sit; she just simply cannot sit any longer. "All day long I have to sit at school," she complains as her mother leads her back to her seat from near the window. "I need to do

this when I eat or I just can't eat!" Jessica exclaims, hanging upside down from her chair, attempting to stuff a piece of broccoli into her mouth. "You can choke that way!" her mother exclaims, grabbing the broccoli and taking away her plate. "When you are ready to sit and eat your dinner safely, you can have your plate back."

OK, remember our **Push Your Wiggles!** super power? We're going to learn a new one where we don't push the wiggles, we **squeeze** them; kind of like an orange that we are turning into juice. Just like before, take all of your wiggles, starting at your toes and going all the way to your head. Now, hold them in your fists. Have them? Raise your right foot when you do. Now, squeeze those wiggles in your hands until they disappear. Great job!

Do you think our **Squeeze Your Wiggles!** super power was enough to help Jessica eat her dinner safely? Let's find out…

Super Power #10: Squash Your Wiggles!

Do you like recess? Nah, I'll bet you really don't like that. All that playing, running around? You'd rather, um, eat brussel sprouts. I'm not knocking brussel sprouts, though, they are pretty delicious.

I'm kidding about the recess thing. Recess is so much fun, isn't it? Did you ever feel like you just never wanted to come back inside, and just keep running and playing? Touch your left knee if you've felt that way. I sure have; but with me, it was flying, not running. Not to brag or anything.

Hmmm, let's see what's going on with Jack. Make sure your detective hat is on nice and tight. Is it? Great!

Jack is at recess. He is climbing up the monkey bars. He is so high! He swings from one to the next. Wow! He spots a group of friends playing tag. He zooms over, joining in and darting quickly away from the tagger. He is so fast, nobody can catch him! "Ring," the bell sounds. Recess is over. One by one, Jack's friends leave the courtyard, grabbing their lunchboxes as they line up. But Jack just can't stop running! "Woo hoo!" He laughs, running around the now-empty courtyard. "You need to line up right now," the recess teacher says, walking over to him. "But I can't stop running!" Jack says. "I mean it!"

Wow, we were just talking about that! I know just how to help. Let's learn the super power of **Squash Your Wiggles!** Take all of your wiggles, starting from your toes and going all the way up to your head. Do you have all of them? Great! Now, hold them like a big ball of wiggles between your hands. Ready? Now, push your hands together and **squash squash squash** the wiggles until they are gone! You did it!

I have a good feeling about this one. Do you think our **Squash Your Wiggles!** super power helped Jack get back in line with his class?

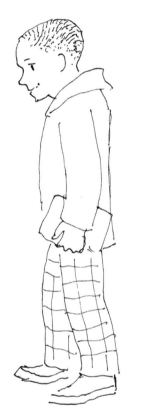

Super Power #11: Cocoon!

Are you getting a little wiggly as you are listening to the book? If you are, why don't you try one of the super powers we just learned? Remember how we practiced the three below?

- **Push Your Wiggles!**
- **Squeeze Your Wiggles!**
- **Squash Your Wiggles!**

Do you need some help remembering how to do these super powers? That's OK, ask your helpful reader to remind you. They are super-awesome and would love to help you.

OK, moving on to our next kid who needs our help...let's meet Joel.

Joel is sitting at the kitchen table. He knows he is supposed to be doing his reading homework, but it is so hard to just sit and work when his mom is on the phone, his brother is eating dinner next to him, and he can't even feel his body anymore! "I am just too tired to read, mom," Joel calls out. "I can't even sit. I'll read later, OK?" Joel throws his book down onto the table and starts jumping up and down on the couch. "Stop jumping and get back to your work!" his mom says, a tinge of annoyance in her voice. "No!" Joel replies, jumping higher and faster.

Do you get homework yet? Even if you don't, I'll bet you can understand the feeling of just not wanting to sit anymore, huh? Have you ever felt so wiggly or so tired that you couldn't even feel your body anymore? That's a hard question, I know. Take a minute to think about it. You may not even know the answer, and that's OK.

For this next super power, we are going to need space on the floor. Get ready for our next super power, **Cocoon**.

First, get on your hands and knees. Next, **cradle** your head in your arms and curl your body into a tight, tight ball. You can do this with your belly facing the floor, or to the side. Now, picture where in your body you feel your wiggles the most. Do you feel them in your feet? Your arms? Your neck? Or are they all over your body? Now, squeeze those wiggles out of your body until they disappear. Ahhh…so much better!

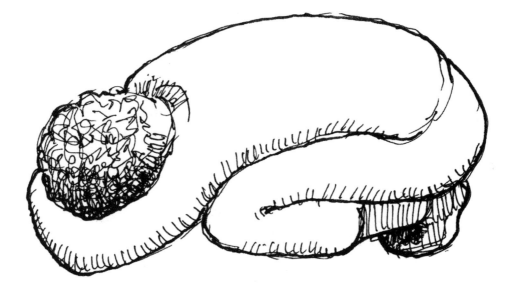

What do you think? Did we help Joel finish his reading homework? Turn the page and find out.

Anger Management

All of the scenes that we are going to look at now have kids who feel **angry**. Do you know what "anger" means? When someone feels angry, they feel a warning inside that something is wrong. When you are angry, you feel very, very, upset. Some part of you may even feel threatened. The feeling of anger is physical (in your body) and in your mind (how you think about what is making you angry).When you feel angry, your heart may beat fast, your muscles may feel tight, and your breathing may be fast, too. Your thoughts may be going too quickly to even think!

Do you have a tip that has worked for you when you felt this way? What made you feel better? If you feel comfortable sharing this, wave your right arm up quietly. That will show the grownup reading this book that you want to talk about it.

Super Power #12: Stop Sign!

Woo-hoo! You are on your way, Self-Controls in training! You are unstoppable, kids! This next one will be a cinch for you.

Still have your detective hat and magnifying glass? Great! We're going to need them to help us solve this case.

Let's look at the picture.

Class 1A is buzzing with the sounds of laughter, music, and happy talking. Blocks are being stacked into a large and towering city by Jack and Lenny. Dina and Ronnie are busy being teacher's helpers, and Linda and Shani are over by the art center looping paper chains. Melissa glances over to the center of the room. Aviva, Daniel, Jack, and Ben are all dancing there, smiling and laughing together. "I'm such a bad dancer," Melissa thinks. "I can't go over there. Besides, they

are having so much fun without me. They are just leaving me out. They don't even notice that I am all alone!"

OK, let's learn the next super power! When you get **angry**, you may just want to yell, scream, cry, or use your body in a way that may not be kind or safe. Guess what? This super power can help you to stop and get back in control! Let's try it. This new super power is called **Stop Sign!**

Close your eyes. Picture in your head your very own "**STOP**" sign. What colors does it contain? What shape is it? What does it feel like? Now, once you have it in your mind, tell yourself quietly, "**STOP**." Do you know how to count to ten? Now, try counting slowly: 1, 2, 3, 4, 5, 6, 7, 8, 9, 10.

Great! Let's see if the strength of our **Stop Sign!** super power helped Melissa feel better. Turn the page.

Super Power #13: Make a List!

I may be getting my vacation time earlier than I thought! Who knew you were such fast learners? Are you sure that you didn't already go to Self-Control school? Yes? Hmmm, OK…if you're sure…remind me to find out what you eat for breakfast, then. It must be really great for your brain. I should add it to my grocery list.

Brush off your detective hat and wipe your magnifying glass clean! We're going to need them to help us solve this next tricky case. I like the confident faces I'm seeing! We can do it!

Kingston, we're on our way, buddy!

Kingston did not clean up the toys in his room. "I'm sorry, honey, but now you can't go for the playdate with Timothy this afternoon," his mother says. "That's so mean! I'm tired! It's too many toys, I can't do it!" *Kingston yells, flopping down onto his bed.*

OK, let's learn the next super power! When you get angry there may be lots of different problems piling into your head all at once. Wouldn't it feel better to get them out? That's where this next super power comes in! It's called **Make a List!**

Close your eyes. Take a deep breath. Take a moment and think: *Is there anything that is on my mind that is making me feel* **overwhelmed** *and* **angry**? Picture a paper and pen, pencil, crayon, or marker in your mind. Silent thumbs up when you've got it. Now, write or draw out each problem on that paper in your mind. Fold it up. You can always come back to it later, if you still need it.

Great! Let's see if the strength of our **Make a List!** super power helped Kingston feel better. Turn the page.

Emotional Regulation

All of the scenes that we are going to look at now have kids who feel what I like to call **yucky feelings**. Yep, you heard me right. I said **yucky feelings**, which are those bad, sad, mad, hurt, make-you-want-to-cry feelings. Everybody gets them. But just like every other chapter of this book, guess what? There is something that we can do about them. That's where our super powers come in!

Do you have a tip that has worked for you when you felt any of these **yucky feelings**? What made you feel better? If you feel comfortable sharing this, blink your eyes three times. That will show the grownup reading this book that you want to talk about it.

Super Power #14: Take Yourself to a Peaceful Place Inside!

Wow, mini-superstars! We are approaching graduation! You have mastered almost all of the super powers! Can I call you when my beeper goes off? Perfect. Listen for my call, or watch for my fly-by. You rock!

Maggie is very overwhelmed. Her friends in school did not want to sit with her during lunch, her teacher told her that she was not listening, and now her brother was touching her hair and laughing! It was just too much! She just hit him! She was just so mad! "Go to your room!" Maggie's mom exclaims. "We use our words, not our hands." Her hands in fists, shoulders hunched, she yells at her mother, "That is so not fair! You only see what I do...he never gets in trouble!"

Here's a Self-Control fact: I have a little sister. Guess what? I *always* felt like she got away with *everything*, and I was the one who *always* got in trouble. This made me even *angrier*, which got me in trouble *again*, so I was in trouble a lot. Can you relate to this feeling? If you can, clap three times and touch your nose.

Time to learn one of our last super powers: **Take Yourself to a Peaceful Place Inside!**

In between long flights, and when I am feeling very overwhelmed, I sometimes take myself to an imaginary place, a beautiful place that is peaceful to me. It is sometimes a happy moment, or a story that I re-tell myself. This is my favorite super power—**Take Yourself to a Peaceful Place Inside!** Let's try it!

Close your eyes. Breathe in and out slowly. Focus on hearing the sound of your breath going in and out. Now, that sound is going to take you to a magical place, a secret land called *Calmtopia*. Stretch out your arms. You are now floating, with twinkling stars above and below you. A shooting star passes by your eyes, casting a trail of glitter across your face.

Suddenly, a tunnel appears in the middle of the night sky, swirling purple, blue, and green, and you swim into it, feeling warm and cozy, as it gently pushes you onto a white fluffy cloud. It is soft and squishy, like a marshmallow. You sink into it, feeling cuddled and light. You are now in Calmtopia. The sky is a sparkling blue, with little dancing rainbows scattered across the horizon. You can almost reach out and touch them!

You realize that your cloud is slowly sinking, stopping at a bubbling brook surrounded by purple and blue flowers. They smell so sweet, you can almost taste them. The grass feels so soft on your bare toes and fingers. When the clouds on the horizon clear, you see a silver-and-gold castle appear, with sparkling steps made out of gems sprouting out of the ground in front of you. You take a step, feeling the cool jewels under your bare feet. You make your way to the castle. The old wooden doors open with a soft creak, and you cautiously step inside.

A room appears, its walls royal blue, a golden table in its center. A single note lay next to a jar of sparkling glitter on the table. The note reads:

Welcome to the Castle of Calm and Peace. Close your eyes. Picture in your mind all of the hopes and dreams that you have for yourself. Do you want to be confident? Then be confident. Do you want to be in control? Then don't just wish it, make it so. Grab a handful of glitter, and repeat those hopes for yourself. When you are ready, open your eyes. Just remember, remind yourself of this place and of those dreams that you made for yourself today. You may even find a speck of glitter left on your clothes.

Now, open your eyes. How do you feel? Let's hope our new super power, **Take Yourself to a Peaceful Place Inside!**, helped Maggie. Turn the page and we will find out.

Super Power #15: Give Yourself a Head Massage!

Oh my goodness! We are now up to our very last super power. I can't believe it. I can't wait to show it to you.

Let's help out our last kid in need for the day, shall we?

Harry has been waiting for two whole weeks for this sleepover, and it's finally happening. Sam is over, and they are watching a movie in comfy pajamas and eating snacks after regular bedtime. It's perfect. Well, it's perfect until Harry's big brother comes and sits right between them. "Why are you watching this movie? Why don't you play catch instead? I'll start!" "Sure!" Sam replies, leaving Harry alone on the couch. "But I don't like catch," Harry says to them. "I want to keep watching the movie." "So you can watch it yourself while we play, right, Sam?" His brother runs off with Sam. Tears well up in Harry's eyes until they finally spill over. "This is the worst sleepover ever!" He thinks, going into his room and shutting the door. "They won't even notice that I went to bed."

Have you ever felt sad? Lonely? Left out? I have, and it doesn't feel nice. But guess what? There's something that we can do to change those feelings, even if we can't always change other people. I will always remember my own mom telling me when I would feel this way, "Self-Control, you can't change other people, and you can't change many situations, but you can change your feelings and how you react." She's a smart lady.

Want to know something to do with the **yucky feelings** we were just talking about? This brings us to our very last super power, **Give Yourself a Head Massage!** Seriously.

Close your eyes. Picture where in your brain those **yucky thoughts** are. Touch your right knee with your left elbow when you've found those thoughts. Now, put your left hand on the left side of your head and your right hand on the right side of your head. Rub, rub, rub the yucky feelings out of your brain until they disappear. Amazing! And it feels nice, too.

I hope that we helped Harry turn that sleepover around! Let's find out...

You Made it, Kid!

Congratulations! You have earned the official **"Self-Control graduation diploma!"** Now that you have learned how to use my super powers, I shouldn't be seeing you on my **"self-control** alarm watch," right?

Maybe one day, with enough practice, you can earn one of your own watches. But that's for another book, maybe—if I can find enough time to write in between all the calls I get.

Well, that's up to you, though, partly. *Practice, practice, practice.* If enough kids practice self-control, and use some of these way cool super powers, then maybe I will have enough time to write my next book to share even more amazing secrets.

I may even find the time to chow down on some take-out on a Sunday, or pop by at your house, school, or even play date one day when you *least* expect me!

Self-Controls, to the rescue!

PART 2

FOR ADULTS

Tips to Make the Most of the Activities and Strategies in This Book

Take a Deep Breath

When I work with children, I find that using actual bubbles is a great way to give them a concrete way to see the right and wrong way to take a good, deep breath. Before reading this section, you can demonstrate yourself what happens when you breathe too hard, too fast, and with not enough air. Then, let the child have a turn. To incorporate self-control into the activity, I like to say, "You may not pop the bubbles, just look at how beautiful they are as they fall," or "You can only pop the bubbles you blow, not anyone else's bubbles."

Make a Mantra

Some children may benefit from creating a visible tool, at least initially, that they can utilize on a daily basis, with a mantra that you would like them to internalize. This can be written/represented pictorially/visually on a bracelet, bookmark, post-it note, key ring, etc. You can place this mantra in many places throughout the home and school settings so that the child can begin to internalize the message. They should be the one to choose the mantra, in order to gain internal meaning and gratification from this strategy.

Use Your Words

Kids may have different reasons for not using their words when they are experiencing a strong emotion. This may be due to a developmental difficulty, a medical diagnosis, a learned behavior, or a combination of things. Providing children with alternative ways to express themselves (e.g. a visual chart to express things such as "I feel…" or "I need…"), and allowing them to choose, may be a good option. Providing them with an "I need a break" card when you are seeing warning signs that they are beginning to lose control is another strategy. Creating a safe space in your house or classroom where they can take a moment to regroup (usually, pairing this with a visual timer is a good idea) will allow them to get their thoughts in order, so that they can use their words, whether that is internal (thinking more clearly) or external (with you or another "helpful grownup"). Remember, using words is a difficult skill, and some children may need additional processing time for word retrieval.

Just Give Yourself a Hug

This is one of my favorite physical self-regulatory strategies from my first books, and a simple way for young children to get deep-pressure input on their own, relying less on adult intervention. Deep pressure, or proprioceptive input, provides the body with information about where it is in space, and is a quick and simple way for a child to feel safe, comforted and self-regulated. On that note, it is very important that all children receive regular deep-pressure and other sensory-based movement times throughout their day, in order to stay regulated. This keeps their neurological systems, including their "cup of coping chemicals" in their brain, full and able to manage what daily life throws at them. Whether you are a parent, teacher, or therapist, it is important to realize that children need the opportunity to engage in these opportunities, and cannot be expected to sit and complete sedentary and often cognitive-based tasks without the opportunity for movement. Examples of types of movement are:

- Give Yourself a Hug

- Cross Crawls

- Jumping Jacks

For detailed information on more movement breaks, you can check out my first book, *The Kids' Guide to Staying Awesome and in Control: Simple Stuff to Help Children Regulate their Emotions and Senses*, and take a look at my website at www.awesomeandincontrol.com.

Crumple Up Your Worries

To introduce this activity and make it more concrete, you may want to first complete the pencil-to-paper task, that is, take a marker and a piece of paper (providing the child with the opportunity of choice here as much as possible) and have them physically write or draw all of their worries. Once they are finished, allow them to actually crumple up the paper and throw it away. This process may make this super power more concrete.

Throw Away Your Worries

You may want to complete a tangible activity prior to learning this specific super power. For example, you may want to try utilizing soft physical items, such as pompoms or cotton balls, having your child name each worry as they pick up each item. Next, have the child collect them all and throw these tangible worries away to a specified location of their choice. As an alternative, you may want to do the following to go into more depth: Have them look around the room, and ask them, "Where is a good place that you would want to throw away your worries? Where do you feel your worries the most? What color are your worries? Can you picture them in your mind?" Have them draw a picture of themselves (full body) utilizing different-colored crayons, markers, etc., and have them draw the areas of their body where they feel their worries the most, and what color(s) those worries are.

Make a Worry Box

To make this super power more tangible for some children, you may want to do an activity of creating an actual worry box. This could be a tangible tool that is used throughout the day, or just as a preview to learning about this specific super power. Creating a worry box could be as simple as utilizing an empty tissue box (and decorating it with markers), or as complex as utilizing a wooden box from a crafts store and painting it, and utilizing an actual small lock. In terms of naming actual worries, you may either want to utilize small manipulatives, such as cotton balls or pompoms (or another item of choice), or simply have the child picture the worries in their mind, as described in the book, and "place" them in the box.

Push Your Wiggles

When children engage in this activity, they are providing deep pressure to the body while also crossing the midline. This provides a calming effect on the nervous system and allows for the two hemispheres of the brain to "talk to each other," improving focus, as well.

Squeeze Your Wiggles

This is the same as Squash Your Wiggles but with different hand movements. In order to make this super power more tangible, you can cut out squares of bubble wrap. Have the child hold one piece of bubble wrap in each hand. Explain that this represents their wiggles, and that when they squeeze the bubble wrap, the wiggles will disappear! The audible popping noise should reinforce the message. To differentiate this even further, you can purchase the large bubble wrap and have the child draw or write out a representative drawing on the bubble itself. Once they squeeze the bubble and it pops, what they drew or wrote will actually disappear.

Squash Your Wiggles

In order to make this super power more tangible (and this can be quite fun, as well, but pretty messy), you can have the child take something small and squishy carefully between their palms (a tomato, a peeled orange, etc.), with their hands over a bin or a bucket. Explain that this item represents their wiggles, and when they are squishing them, their wiggles are turning into juice and disappearing!

Cocoon

This is one of my favorite yoga positions that I often use in my clinical practice as a therapist. It is grounding, as much of the body touches the floor while the child is actively hugging and squeezing themselves into a ball, providing deep pressure throughout the body, with their eyes closed so that their attention is focused inward. This is a great gross motor and sensory integrative exercise to utilize before having a child sit for a prolonged period of time, or when a child is feeling extremely dysregulated.

Stop Sign

If you would like a more tangible way to remind the child of this important super power, a good tool/strategy would be to simply sketch a stop sign. (Either you could do this or have the child complete this independently or contribute, which would provide ownership over the tool.) The stop sign should be small enough to fit on a key ring, so that you can clip it to the child's belt loop as a reminder throughout their day.

Make a List

To introduce this activity and make it more concrete, you may want to first complete the pencil-to-paper task, that is, take a marker and a piece of paper (providing the child with the opportunity of choice here as much as possible) and have them write or draw each problem that they have on their mind on that paper. Next, have them fold up the paper. Remind them that they can always come back to it later, if they need. This process may make this super power more concrete.

Take Yourself to a Peaceful Place Inside

This may be my favorite strategy of the entire book. The world that we live in is so "plugged in" to all the technology out there, with the smartphones, tablets, media, etc. That's not to say that I am not a fan of the iPad (I often use it in my practice!); I just find it important that children (and adults!) get—and take—the opportunity to "unplug" and come back to themselves. In this particular section of the book, where Self-Control teaches children the super power of **"Take Yourself to a Peaceful Place Inside,"** we are truly addressing the strategy of cognitive flexibility, imaginative thinking, as well as meditation, sustained attention, and mindfulness. This can be as simple as thinking of a positive memory, or using the meditation story *Calmtopia* as a script. If you read it routinely and consistently, it becomes a part of your child's "coping toolbox." I work with a student, let's call her MJ. I have been doing a lot of these types of meditation stories with her at the end of our treatment sessions. As I stated in this part of the book, this can be as simple as thinking of a positive memory or using the meditation story that I wrote. If you read it often enough, it becomes a part of the child's "coping toolbox." I work with a particular student and have been doing a lot of meditation stories with her at the end of our treatment sessions. One day, as she was leaving my office, she turned to me and said, "Ms. Lauren, you have to tell my mom about these stories. I woke up from a nightmare, and instead of going into my mom's bed, I remembered the story you have been telling me, and I told it to myself and went back to bed!" Wow, what an "I-love-my-job" kind of moment. (Tip: You can dim the lights and play very peaceful music in the background while you read the story.)

Give Yourself a Head Massage

A way to make this super power more concrete is to have the child first draw a self-portrait, with only the head and neck showing. Next, they should draw different thought bubbles coming from their head, sketching or writing out different **yucky feelings** about which they are thinking. Now, have them rub their temples and/or the top of their head. Finally, have them "X" out each yucky feeling as it disappears.

Reminder Bracelets

The bracelets on the next page will reinforce the 15 super powers/strategies learned in this book. You can download the bracelets from www.jkp.com/catalogue/book/9781849057172. Children should wear them daily, with fading prompts from adults, which should, over time, transform these strategies into habits across different environments. The bracelets are divided according to the five sections in this book.

Directions

1. Download and cut out the strips.

2. Photocopy them to utilize them daily.

3. Option 2 (preferred): Laminate a bracelet and circle the preferred super power that you or the child chooses. This creates a durable bracelet that the child can utilize daily.

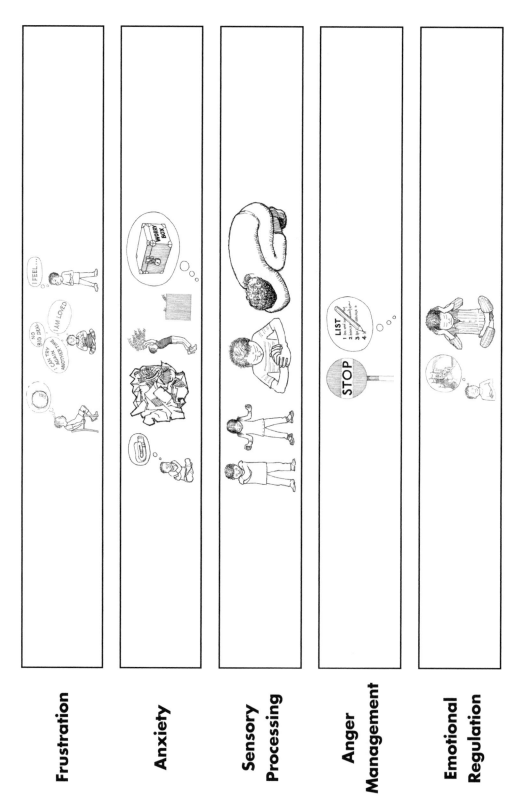

Frustration

Anxiety

Sensory Processing

Anger Management

Emotional Regulation

Self-Control Certificate for

_____

(Fill in the Specific Super Power)

CONGRATULATIONS!

You Have Mastered the Super Power of

_____

Date:_____
Adult Signature:_____
Self-Control Signature: Self-Control

Self-Control Diploma for Knowing All 15 Super Powers!

CONGRATULATIONS on Graduating from Self-Control's Superhero School!

You Are Now an Official Self-Control Hero!

Date:_____

Adult Signature:_____

Self-Control Signature: Self-Control

Desk Strip/Table Strip Reminders

These strips can be downloaded from www.jkp.com/catalogue/book/9781849057172, photocopied or laminated, and placed on a rug, at a desk/table, or on the wall, as a visual reminder of the 15 super power strategies learned in this book. They are divided according to the five sections in this book.

Frustration

Anxiety

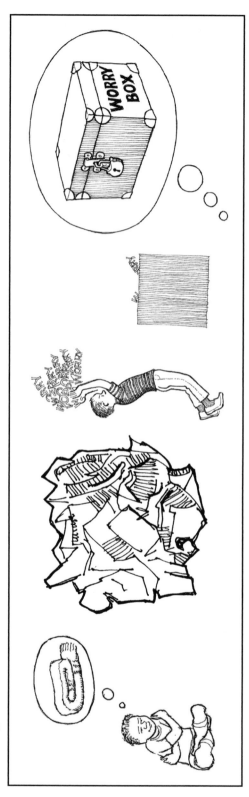

Sensory Processing

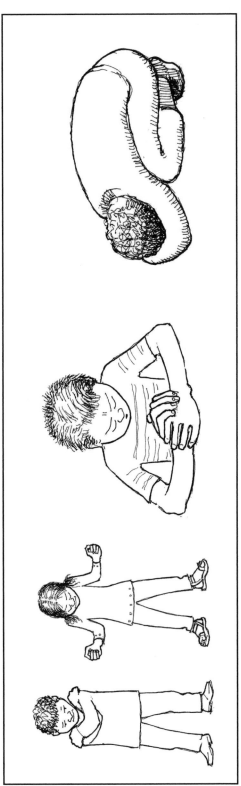

Anger Management

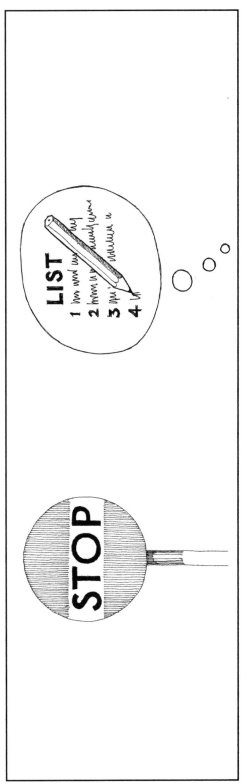

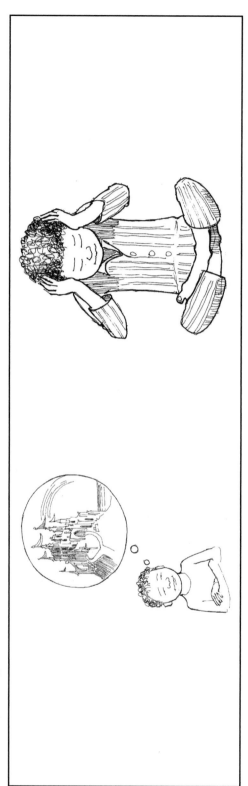

"At a Glance" Reminder Charts

These charts correspond to each key point (i.e. super power) and address each physical or emotional state of regulation (geared toward children but accessible for adults). You can download the charts from www.jkp.com/catalogue/book/9781849057172.

Frustration

Take a Deep Breath!	Make a Mantra!
Use Your Words!	

Anxiety

Just Give Yourself a Hug!	Crumple Up Your Worries!
Throw Away Your Worries!	Make a Worry Box!

Sensory Processing

Push Your Wiggles!		Squeeze Your Wiggles!	
Squash Your Wiggles!		Cocoon!	

Anger Management

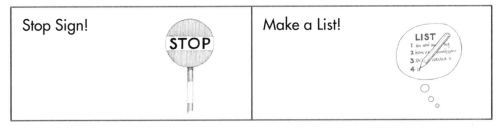

Stop Sign!	STOP	Make a List!	LIST

Emotional Regulation

Take Yourself to a Peaceful Place Inside!		Give Yourself a Head Massage!	